Book One of the Series
Circles of Grace

Compass

To Find my Way

Original poetry

by

Arnolda May Brenneman

© 2018 by Arnolda May Brenneman. All rights reserved. No part of this publication may be reproduced, stored in a retrieval system, or transmitted in any form or by any means – for example, electronic, photocopy, and recording – without the prior written permission of the publisher.

In His Shadow Creations Publications, Lancaster, PA 17603

General Editor: Jan T. Brenneman

Cover design: Jan T. Brenneman

ISBN-13: 978-1986797559

Printed in the United States of America.

nightwriterpoet@gmail.com

Dedication

I dedicate *Compass* in memory of my mother, Bonnie-May Cecile Clocksin, and my father, Paul Preston Clocksin, who together provided a safe and loving home for me and my seven brothers.

My parents' ethical standards and authentic faith were invaluable to fostering emotional stability and spiritual direction for my life.

Table of Contents

Dedication 7
Table of Contents 8
Foreword 1
Part I Listening to Learn 3
   Listen 5
   Find Me There 6
   One Brisk Walk 8
   Marinade 12
   Teach Me 13
   Walkabout 15
   Puzzle Master 19
   Israel 20
   Abba's Call 22
   Off Days and Days Off 23
   Appeal to the Wisdom of the Ages 24
   Time Keepers 27
   Possibilities 28
Part II Nature Speaks 30
   May Day 32
   Earth Speaks 33
   A Squirrel's World 34
   Stepping Stones 35
   Written in the Sky 36
   Welcome the Rain 37
   Rainy Day 38
   Ground Hog Day 39
   Fall Silhouettes 39
   Up a Tree 41
   Ostriches and Eagles 42
   Beauty 43
   This Little Sparrow 44

The Lonely Loon	45
Consider the Trees	46
Outside My Window	49
In My Garden	50
Did You Ever Love a Tree?	52
My Back Yard	53
Part III Awakenings	**55**
Four AM	57
Nocturnal Awe	57
Dream Away	58
Aflame	61
Reflections	62
When Beauty Came	62
Dance of Dawn	63
Dream Dance	64
Prince of Peace	66
In the Spirit	67
Glory Bourne	68
Life Force	68
A World Too Small	70
Part IV Apprehended by Truth	**72**
Prophesy, Oh Painting	74
The Unseen Friend	75
Inside a Day	76
The Stupid Lies I Thought Were True	77
Commutation	79
Ark	80
Messy Love	81
Time Traveler	83
A Painted Poem	90
Teach Me, Abba	92

Two Trees	97
#1 Toxic Thought:, "I Am Not Loved"*	102
And It Was So	103
Spirit Journey	105
Free of the Web	106

Part V In the Light of His Glory 110

The Giving Well	112
In Praise of Christ	113
I Will Praise	114
Pray!	115
I Testify	119
Bring Your Offerings	123
Oh, For the Love of God	123
All for the Glory of God	125
What Kind of Love?	127
Life inside Christ	128
Providence Beckons Me	129
Wellspring	132
Forgiven	133
Perichoresis	134
Other Books in the Circles of Grace Series	137
Children's Poetry Series	138

Foreword

Compass is a poetry book about expanding awareness of direction in life. I write of a growth process based upon observing and listening to nature in a way that is sensory and experiential. In the midst of this is also a spiritual awakening—an awareness of living in an eternal realm that goes beyond the here and now, beyond what I can fully comprehend, but of which I can partake by a life of faith in God.

Part I

Listening to Learn

Listen

Silence stirs in still atmospheres.
It hovers under snow covers of winter,
And beckons the listener draw near.

Hearken closely to its whispers
Surely if you listen you will hear, for the
Silence will speak loudly in your ear.

2014

Find Me There

Find me there
Under the tree, day dreaming;
Looking up into the sky,
Asking all the questions why
And pondering the answers.

Find me there
Near grasses and flowers,
Touching the earth,
Feeling the breeze on my face,
Reveling in the day.

Find me there
Sniffing roses,
Avoiding their thorns;
Discovering songs
In the world all around me.

Find me there
With pen in hand
And scribblings wandering;
Catching words that float by
Like dandelion seeds in summer sky.

Find me there
In small pools reflecting,
Dipping in my feet
And gathering pebbles,
A gem in every one.

Find me there
On low leafy limbs,
Drawn to the tree tops
By flowers, and nests and
Tree living things.

Find me there
Crying for joy,
Laughing in sorrow;
Delight for the day,
Ideas for tomorrow.

Find me there
Taken to another place,
Far above any rat race;
Catching butterflies
And letting them go.

2011

One Brisk Walk

One brisk walk
And a thousand thoughts come to me;
One brisk walk
And the world opens up to me;

From still enclosures and stagnant air
To somewhere, anywhere –
My buoyant legs take me there
Like a spring sprung from its latch.

One brisk walk to watch and see
The movement of life surround me;
The comings and goings, ins and outs;
The smiles and pouts of the people.

Away from the dark and din
Of silent, closed in spaces,
To look into the faces, into the races
Of the weaves and merging around me.

One brisk walk
And my mind opens up;
One brisk walk
And my heart becomes large in me.

Past the sullied sidewalks,
Concrete, glass and steel,
My senses still begin the weal;
My thoughts are freed from concealing.

The sky is my ceiling;
My eyes are the door
That open to places
Not traveled before.

One brisk walk
Is all it may take
To awaken the sleeper inside
And to make the weeper arise.

Soft sunrise, and softer still
The silent moon;
Holding hands with sun and moon
Can make a spirit swoon

In one brisk walk,
In any season of life,
On any day or night,
Will help me walk upright;

Will help me stand and fight
The dirge of shallow and small;
The urge to put up a wall,
With courage to follow a call.

One brisk walk
To breathe the air clean;
To discover a dream
In the making.

Continued...

To gather the gold
For the taking;
To find a force in me,
Making me smile inside;

Making me wide
From narrow thinking;
Making me glide
On legs unslinking

On one brisk walk
Through country or town,
Changing my frown
Till I'm clowning around;

Turning the ebb to a flowing;
The numb to a knowing;
The dim perspectives
To a glowing of light

In one brisk walk

2013

Marinade

Let me soak in the music
    To nourish my soul,
Or sit by the seaside
    To watch the waves roll.
There is a part of me
    Not confined to the nine till five;
A part of me beyond daily grind.
    It is where I unwind
From the corkscrew tensions,
    And I color outside the lines.

A part of me must wander
    And get lost in a universe
That awes and inspires me;
    That draws and replenishes;
That requires my trustful abandon;
    That washes me with its billow
Of comfort beyond cushions and pillows
    And peace beyond treaties,
And safety beyond walls
    And security like the babe at breast knows.

2012

Teach Me

Show me the school in the country
Where learning grows as naturally as trees.
Take me to the college out of doors
Where knowledge is gathered like honey by bees.

Lead me on real life adventures
Beyond the newspaper, internet, and TV.
Guide me down winding pathways
Where I glean berries on the way;

Where I collect in my basket
All the marvels of a fresh new day;
Where I see, touch, hear, taste, smell
And take time to think about it all;

Where the cognate is a whole,
Not in dismembered parts;
Where experience is unified;
Not in isolated compartments.

Take me to the land of books,
To learn where other lives have trodden;
School me in the lessons of history
That dare not be forgotten.

Let me read them first hand;
To listen to others, while thinking for myself.
Let me expand in my understanding,
As yesterday's knowing will not suffice.

Help me not to settle for beans and rice
When there is a banquet of learning for me.
Grace me to integrate the facts that I glean
Into meaningful existence.

Prod me to move on and explore
Before complacency finds a place in me.
Keep me humble to admit my ignorance;
To position myself as a student in life.

Take me to that Beulah land
Where I can stand and see afar off;
To feast my eyes on the beauty surrounding me
And my school that reaches from sea to sea.

2011

Walkabout

I often walk alone—
The streets, the park, the beach;
In the sun, in the cold,
In the wind, in the breeze;
Kicking random stones,
Gazing into sunsets;
Studying the clouds;
Touching trees with leaves;
Watching flowers with bees;
Catching butterflies fluttering;

Or viewing people weave through streets.
Not so many smiling faces do I see,
But some, perchance I meet
To exchange a glance suddenly
And suddenly retreat again
To my sole pedestrian role;
As roll by the cars with strangers,
Encased within their private chambers
Of rapid transportation,
While I mosey along, on foot.

Neighbors sit on steps and porches,
Where babies have crept and elderly snored;
The jolly laughed, the downcast wept;
And all is fleeting, swept away in time.
Some residents ignore me, and
Others wait for my routine greeting,
Because they are all alone
And it warms a lonely heart
To be noticed on a city street
Where folks pass by but seldom meet.

I walk among the busy shops
And watch society in all its roles;
The homeless stroll aimlessly,
Not sure where they are going,
While businessmen and women
Walk erect, directly to their goals,
With fists clenching their brief cases
Filled with doubtless precious papers
Or purses packed with paper money,
Not backed by gold or silver.

The people filter in and out,
And I am their unobtrusive observer,
That is, unless someone is
Unobtrusively watching me ...
But no, they are too busy
It always seems,
And when I picture such scenes
It is as if people go about
Their daily business in a hazy dream
And aren't quite fully living—

At least, that is how it looks to me,
When they argue over little things
And call each other fowl names,
Or spit carelessly where others walk,
And I think when this day is gone,
We all have one day less to live;
So isn't there a little more
We all can give to the world?
For we all can make a difference—
Every man and woman, boy and girl   *Continued...*

Thinking all these things, my mind
Goes in a swirl, whirling from
This present place to a knowing;
To a consciousness growing
That our journey on earth is short
And our visitation here is veering near—
So very near, we cannot know—
To a transcendent quality of eternity,
Of which we are often unaware,
Yet we share this pilgrimage.

So, I go on my excursions; cataloging
In my searching mind the many versions
Of my foot trails, and the scenes I've left behind;
Placing in my mental files,
The many miles I've walked alone;
I hide in my soul the people, the places,
The smiles, the faces, everywhere I go.
They are stored in unforgettable memory,
Etched in my bones. I take them all home,
And I realize I never did walk alone.

2012

Puzzle Master

This earthly zeal;
Is like spinning my wheels;
Or driving on a near empty tank.

Pieces don't fit,
And I've just got to quit
And give it to the Puzzle Master.

I play the fool
If I try to improve
On the Operator's Instructions.

My wheels would rust,
And without simple trust
I could not figure half of it out;

No reason to pout;
When I give Him the wheel,
It's the wind in my face that I feel.

2012

Israel

Israel, you speak to me;
You talk to me;
You whisper in my ear.

As you reveal your history,
My vision becomes clear;
Your people become dear.

Israel, you teach me,
Embrace me, enlarge me;
You draw me near.

You deepen me;
Quicken me;
I feel your heartbeat.

You show me your art
In design and
Patterns and hues.

You fit me with shoes
To walk your landscape
And see your fame.

I hear the Good News
In spite of your desert
And wilderness dunes.

I swim in your seas;
And walk through your waters;
I'm baptized anew.

I gaze at your beauty;
I feel your glory;
I stand here and muse.

Israel, written in the stars,
Carved in the land,
Held in God's hand;

Apple of His eye,
Yeshua, your guide,
Brings me home.

2010

Abba's Call

Come away, come away
To quiet, solitary places.
Come away from the many faces
Of mere humanity,
For a season, for a time;
For a respite, for a while.

Find me at the Sabbath;
Meet me in the rest,
And I will sustain you
For the tests that lay before you.
Drink your fill
Till dusk meets dawn

And all the cares and clutter
Are wondrously gone
From the landscape of your soul.
Make this your goal:
To meet me there
In the holy tabernacle

Of me and you and the angels.
Then I will send you out again
Full and satisfied;
Satiated and overflowing.
Come away, come away, again;
Come away with my friend.

2012

Off Days and Days Off

If I'm sick I stay home; I read a book;
I take another look out my window
And see things differently, and
I say, "It's okay; time's not lost on me."

There's more to do in a single day
Than any soul can imagine, but
When I'm bereft of the duties, I'm left
With hidden pleasures to discover.

I take out a notebook and write a while,
Till I find a world inside to uncover.
When the days are quiet and friends are few,
I notice things like morning dew and
Sparrows hidden in the bushes.

I slow down enough to hear the ticking
Of the clock, as when I'm submerged
In a leisurely bath and can hear
The beating of my own heart.

It's a good time to clear out the clutter
That piles up from a too-busy life;
It's a moment to slow down and
Take time to remember;

To allow my mind to ponder the
Treasures I've put on the shelf.
It takes me back to my childhood;
To being a little girl with a world to
Discover and no one to rush me;

To crush the serendipity
Of those off days by saying,
"Hurry up or you'll miss the bus!"

2016

Appeal to the Wisdom of the Ages

Hello, I am the minority;
The oddity in the crowd.
I gather up my courage
And dare to speak out loud.

My words may embarrass;
My concepts sound strange.
It's easy to spot me; and
I'm a target free range.

"Where does she come from?"
"Isn't she awfully young to
Be so old fashioned?"
Perhaps people may say,

"Get with the times; come
Out of the Dark Ages." Yet
I will say, "Give heed to the
Sages and learn what is true."

Wisdom never ages, so let
Its muse wash over us till
Our eyes are young again
And we can see brand new.

History is our pedagogue,
Whose lessons test validity
Of forgone conclusions.
So we gather to be schooled.

We must be tutored in the art
Of thinking things through
And in the craft of releasing
Logical speech based on facts.
We must review to learn anew

What it means to fully listen;
Not just glisten with the gossip
Of the current madding crowd.

We must be silent to be lucid
Before we speak out loud.
For we must wait and hesitate
Before we judge to scold the old.

Time will tell, but until then we
Must train our faculties to listen
Long and listen well, for truth,
Rightly perceived, will reward us.

Resist propaganda! The boom
Of the deafening crowd, versed
By media hounds, to break the curse
Of the all-consuming "now."

Do not ignore generations gone
Before us and their timeless truths;
Nor spurn their priceless sermons
That instruct us to discern.

Let's question our accepted views,
That we not trade the Wisdom of Ages
For the commodity of fools.
When we ask, we utilize the past

We've been given to teach us truth.
We'll see past the present to discover
Eternal good news that does not shift with
The seasons of trendy world views.

2018

Time Keepers

The clock ticks; the cricket chirps, the faucet drips; the puppy licks;
The rain drops, the wipers squeal, the shoes click; hooves clop; the knife chops;
Tired ones plop; the bell tolls; dead leaves crunch; and squirrels munch their lunch;
Bullfrogs croak; rabbits lope into the brush; mosquitoes hover;
Hands slap; horse tails swish; nostrils twitch and the deer dash for cover;

Spoons clink in the sink, children smack snacks—when they lack their manners;
A lamb is bleating, horses chomp while eating; cows chew their cud.
Workman go thud, and rat-a-tat-tat—you need ear plugs for that.
Horns beep, car brakes shriek; tires squeal; puddles splash and leak their stew;
Folks dash past flags at half mast; now all I hear are jack hammers;

Birds cheep; frogs leap and splash; bees buzz; while cats purr and lick their fur;
Fuzzy chicks peep; creeks gurgle and glug; streams gush while leaves glisten;
Hasten to the sounds swirling all around and consider this:
Still your feet and quiet your disposition; Hush, hush; listen;
Beyond these timekeepers all, can you pause to hear your heartbeat?

2017

Possibilities

My world continually brims with possibilities;
Poems and songs that descend as dew from the heavens;
Painted in pastels and oils and watercolors.
Possibilities of bike rides, swimming and dance,
Prancing like playmates in circles around me.

Creation yet awakens in me and beauty yet
Astounds me. Friends of every feature and form surround
Me. I caress the ground; fondle leaves and fronds of ferns.
I learn and learn and learn; from the books abounding;
And I learn through sight and touch and smell and sound.

I listen to silence and I listen to the loud;
To the clouds passing by and to the boast of the proud.
In curiosity I wonder why; and in my
Queries I ask the who and when and where and how?
While I'm down to earth, I continue my search,

But still I dare to reach high for the stars in the sky;
Many years I've been looking for treasures far and near—
Far as the oceans and near as the end of my pen.
Each morning I awaken, I begin again;
Each newborn day extends to me its pleasures.

Each day seems measured by a clock in eternity
That patterns a rhythm like the beating of my heart.
From the start to the end I am presented with vast
Possibilities; and likewise my friend, please do
Attend to my words when I say, so are you.

2017

Part II

Nature Speaks

May Day

If I knock,
And the door does not open;
If I seek,
But can't find what I'm looking for;
If I ask,
But no one answers my request,
Then I'll leave my flowers
On the doorstep,
And if they droop and wither,
So be it,
But perchance
A May-Day seeker
Will find them there
And bloom.

2015

When I was young, my mother told me of an old tradition of placing flowers on your neighbor's doorstep on the first day of May, called May Day.

Earth Speaks

Flowers freely give their scent
And gratis share their colors;
Neither do the birds relent
Their serenade at night or
Wake-up songs in morning.

Apples bend the branches low;
And yield them for our taking,
All the fruit in orchards grow
To satiate our craving;
And all the world is waiting…

The gifts that they bestow so
Generously to the earth—
We can scarce begin to show
Gratitude for what it's worth;
Or listen to its longing…

We do not hear them begging
That we pay them for their charms;
But they are only pleading
That we keep them from all harm
And that we feel their pining …

Giving, charming, bestowing;
Sharing, bending, yielding so;
Serenading and showing
Their beauty for all to know;
For our benefit growing;

But waiting, longing, pining,
And begging our attention;
While weary earth is spinning,
To give it our affection;
Nature pleads our nurturing.

2014

A Squirrel's World

So silently the squirrel slithers up the tree,
And though I spy him, I do not know if he sees me.

He stands stoically staring from his leafy perch,
Watching the world in a wondrous animal way;

Waiting patiently for some object he desires,
While for a moment I seek to enter his world—

Small enough to nestle a squirrel, and
Too large a mystery for me to know.

2015

Stepping Stones

I see stones scattered across the creek,
Bridging end to end, side to side;
Some close together, some far and wide.

I am gingerly stepping, skillfully topping
One stone preceding another
In their virgin archipelagos;

Tremulously landing my footfalls
On flat rock plateaus
And small slanted peaks;

I seek safe passage
Without risk of drifting
Nor shifting through the mire;

All the while admiring
Wild rose, and painted daisies
Lazily lilting in soft breezes,

Caressing the lofty waterfront;
Greeting my gaze with their colors;
Meeting my face with their cheer.

Autumn is ever veering near,
And winter patiently waits,
So, I hesitate in my travel

To hold the summer that's here;
To feel its dear kiss on my cheek;
To peak into a timeless season.

I dance my way across the stream;
I pocket every passing scene,
In my memory bank of dreams.

To draw upon in years to come;
To savor, feel, see and walk again
On their stepping stones,

Long since vanished
In the drift and lull of time;
But this moment is mine forever.

2012

Written in the Sky

Bright,
Overcast day
Dense cover of clouds
Refracting
Light particles,
Highlighting hues of color
Before
The coming of the rain.

2015

Welcome the Rain

Pour down, rain, onto this chilly autumn night.
Lull me with your tappings;
You bring to me the trappings
Of a warm and safe abode.

Beat upon the branches,
Bereft of softening leaves.
Tread upon the pavement
Left with no walking feet.

Splash in muddy puddles;
Wash the dusty window panes;
Form the streams and currents
Cascading down sidewalks and lanes.

Fill the drains and cisterns
That meet under the streets;
Carry the gathering remnants of trash and dead leaves
To the lowest possible plane.

Come down in the night; come down when I sleep;
Come down till you empty the skies;
Saturate the soil and fill the streams;
Clear the fog from the air and debris from the streets.

Come rain, comfort me;
Sing me your lullaby melodies;
Carry me through to the morning;
A glistening and fragrant new day.

2011

Rainy Day

Dayspring
    Fresh
        Newborn

Daytime
    Playtime
Springtime
    New day born

Raindrops
    Spraying
        Pattering
Sprinkling
    Tapping on the morn

Cars splashing
    Puddles thrashing

Splaying droplets
    Raindrops Popping
Spattering

Leaflets turning
    Foliage churning

Boughs bouncing
    Trees Dancing

Grasses gleaming
    Rivulets
        Streaming

Branches wiggling
    Arbor billowing

Soft as pillows
    Wet willows

Weeping water
    Dripping droplets.

Drizzling
    Dripping

Popping
    Tapping

Splashing
    Thrashing

Bouncing
    Prancing

Rainy day

2014

Ground Hog Day

I begin to feel in me
Stirring and awakening;
There are things I've never seen;
It's reality, not dream.

Have I known this place before?
Is there something big in store;
That goes beyond the old lore,
To acquire what is more?

I feel the life rising up,
Like a day that's just begun;
Discovery of a new way,
With the rising of the sun.

2002

Fall Silhouettes

Figures amble towards me;
Willowing motion cascading;
Through sunlight and shady patches;
Bending in tiredness;
Balanced in contraposition,

They're absorbing warm rays
While in the early autumn days,
Somewhere between summer and cold;
Between green and bare,
And highlighted in fall colors.

2012

Up a Tree

Oh, to climb your limbs, majestic tree:
To swing from your branches and
To sway in the breeze, like one
Of your multitudes of leaves that
Look down from their tremulous perch,
Clothing your arms in flutters
As they shake and flitter and lurch.
I would look through your kaleidoscope
And occupy my mind with every lofty

Dream and hope that will not fall,
No matter how strong the wind,
And I would see far and wide
All over the countryside,
Past the normal human scope,
Of two feet planted on the ground—
And seeing not much more than
Does a rabbit or a hound—
And I would feel so brave up there,

Unbridled by any earthly care,
Daring to grasp limbs that bend
But do not break, and though the
Leaves tremble and shake, I will
Take the time to view the land
Spread out for miles away,
Sighted from your stately girth,
Till my earth is larger because
I see beyond the world I saw before.

2015

Ostriches and Eagles

Distant relatives, supposedly—
One so bottom-heavy and uselessly-winged
As to make it invalid as an airborne thing;

The other with spans so far and wide
As to make it glide on currents high.
One so cowardly as to run away and flee,

Whenever dangers appear even faintly;
And he timidly hides his head in the ground,
As if it would change his surroundings.

The eagle sharply sees and swiftly acts,
Gathering all the facts to strategize a plan;
He is an inspiration to mortal man.

Birds live by instinct and not by creed;
Be we, chosen heir of free will,
In spite of wind or storm or chill—

Still we choose who we will be;
And we must learn that we are free;
We are free to be like the ostrich,

Who buries its head in the sand;
To flee all threat and not take command;
And we are free to be like the eagle—

To hold our head high in dignity
And spread our wings so regally.
Birds of a feather flock together

And they are constrained by royal decree;
But we decide with which we will identify;
What kind of person we choose to be.

2012

Beauty

Beauty calls
Beauty gestures
Beauty dances in the streets
Beauty waits
Beauty watches
Beauty gathers beauty to herself
Beauty blossoms
Beauty grows
Beauty knows the secrets of the earth
Beauty comes from secrets of the universe
Beauty drops her seeds upon the earth
Beauty multiplies in song and verse
Beauty celebrates in mirth
And gladdens the hearts of every living soul.

2015

This Little Sparrow

The sparrow has a song within her breast
And no one can bribe or wrest it from her.

She travels far away, and wide she roams
To create in foreign lands her new home.

She thrives in the city, country or town
And she adapts to make the nest her own;

Ushers in morning with melody trill;
Welcomes the springtime in recital thrill;

Adventurous in her fresh beginnings
But still faithful in her routine duties.

She is daily caring for her offspring;
A hov'ring mother of a growing brood;

Blends in with the earth, often unnoticed,
Brings gifts to the world with no ill motive.

2012

The Lonely Loon

A solitary loon sat under the lonely moon
And he longed for the day he would find a way;
To rise up and leave his isolation
To be joined with his relations.

For he was trapped in a secluded niche,
Not quite wide enough for a large
Bird of his kind to take flight;
And such is our common plight;

As we long to leave our closed-in places
And see the faces that we've missed.
Sometimes we are like that loon,
And we sit under the lonely moon

And long for some tomorrow
When we will rise above our sorrow;
To lay aside yesterday's chagrin,
And fly among our fellows once again.

Someday may a happy loon
Fly among his fellows soon.
They'll soar under November's sun,
And fly till the day is done.

Together they'll sing in tune
Under the harvest moon;
Sometimes we are like that loon;
May our someday come so soon.

2012

Consider the Trees

The influence of a tree
May seem quite small to you or me,
But consider here some
Tremendous possibilities.

Roots grown deep anchor its weight,
Granting great stability.
Its shade cools the atmosphere
By somewhere near ten degrees.

Birds flock to locate perches;
Squirrels feed on its branches;
Children play in houses
Upon its lofty limbs.

It forms on ground a round perimeter
Felled with catkins, flowers, nuts and fruit—
Innumerable seeds that carry life
For acres more of trees in suit.

They bring more than just good looks;
From its paper come libraries of books.
From the cradle, to crib, to bed, to casket
We take our rest in frames of wood.

From the carpentry of Oak come
Tables, chairs, canes, a boat;
Trees comply to forms and figures;
On stormy seas keeps mankind afloat.

Do they think or understand?
Can they travel far and wide?
Leading others by command?
Holding hands on every side?

No, none of these at all,
Yet they stand free and tall.
And they have a vital key
In the ecosystem overall.

How much more influence have we,
Who can think and feel and see…
We who grace the face of earth
More than the girth of any tree?

We, who touch a million lives,
Who say ten billion words,
Who think a trillion thoughts;
Whose spirits can't be sold or bought?

We, who carry creativity
In song and dance and poetry.
We, who paint the imagery
Of soul dreams and fantasy.

We send rockets to the moon.
And submarines in depth of sea;
We map out each obscure lagoon,
And measure heights of mountain peaks…

Continued…

We, who seek to understand,
To learn, to grow, to comprehend;
The least of our potentiality
Surpasses life of any tree.

So, I stand tall; I stretch my limbs
Because I'm more than just a whim;
And have more dignity than any tree.
Knowing this makes me feel free.

I must never say, "Poor me,"
For that does not become me;
I must not allow myself to pout;
Instead, I choose let the gloomies out.

There's too much livin', too much givin' for me;
Too much adventure on this journey;
When I come to the nitty gritty,
There's just no room for self pity.

The tree does not complain
Or withhold life from its branches
Or devalue its gifts to the world,
But instructs me in generosity.

If ever you become sadder and sadder,
And start to think your life does not matter,
Lay out under some leafy boughs,
And consider the ways of the tree.

2011

Outside My Window

I look out my window and what do I see?
Beautiful trees looking back at me.
From here on the attic floor, I join them
To look down upon the streets of men,
With their cars splashing on wet pavement;

Their sidewalks bearing folks with dogs,
And bicycling children riding along.
We watch speckled leaves cascading down,
Scattered by the wind, gathering into piles,
As tree limbs dance in the autumn chill.

Dear trees, you are thrill of my yesterdays
And to present day I cherish you still;
From stately pine, before this window of mine—
I jumped over you in your sapling days—
To childhood Cedar friend, affectionately

Peering down on dear old Granny Lilac, yet
Bearing fragrant blossoms each and every spring;
And sweet tiny rose bush planted by my daddy.
You bring me joy, you make me want to sing.
Divinely given gifts, outside this window of mine.

2014

In My Garden

I'm roused from nocturnal slumber,
Awakened for the day that's due;
My garden helps me to remember
All things good and lovely and true.

For I have an interior garden
In which I could stay for hours;
I behold the greenery, and then
Am romanced by the flowers;

I am cheered by an aviary;
Of birds that flit every way;
Entertaining me similarly,
Squirrels and rabbits at play.

In my garden is a waterfall
That can soothe a stricken soul,
I let the streams wash over all,
Until I find myself made whole;

Cleansed from soot of daily living;
Revived in the hour of failing strength;
Filled up so I can keep on giving;
With stamina for the journey's length.

I rest among grasses, leaves and petals
And recline on a carpet of green;
The world inside me becomes all settled
And my landscape is a place serene.

My garden is heaven's gateway;
It becomes my earthly paradise.
Here I read and write, sing and pray.
And listen and learn till I'm wise.

In my garden I find myself again;
I return to my center, my core;
And I know I'll be all right when
I not only survive, but more;

That I can thrive, though the world dies
A thousand deaths every day;
For in my garden, I see with new eyes
What earth can not take away.

In my garden I'm revived to life
While I die to all I could never be;
I let go of that ceaseless strife
And find myself gloriously free.

Into bright realm of possibility
Am I birthed anew every day;
Thus forms my personality
In a grand mysterious way.

I tend my garden carefully
So it may flourish and grow;
For, that which is hidden within me
I want the whole world to know.

2015

Did You Ever Love a Tree?

How stately stands the Cedar Tree
Established long on farmhouse lawn,
Set in front the tall white house,
Displaying its bucolic grace,
Towering in arbor elegance,
Through hazy dusk to early dawn.

How lovingly it lent its outstretched limbs
To my years of childhood play.
Those were days when I was young
And the Cedar tree proved my dear friend,
Holding me ever so protectively through
Tumultuous times of growing up.

How generously does it give to all;
How it patiently endures the storms;
How powerfully it grips the earth,
Yet freely reaches to expanse of sky.
It sways in the changing winds of life,
And its branches dance in the breeze.

I said goodbye when I moved away, and
I never forgot my dear friend, the tree.
It may seem sappy, as a tree can't speak,
Except for the language of the earth,
But wrapping your arms about its girth,
Did you ever say, "I love you," to a tree?

2014

My Back Yard

The woody lawn from dusk to dawn
Awaits my footsteps coming.

The yard is full of weeds and briars
But welcomes me with humming.

Its scraggly grass and fallen leaves
Are not a queen's bed of ease

But it pleases me to be here
Among the city's numbing

Cacophony of urban sounds
Outside my gate a drumming.

Inside my pointed picket fence
Secluded for my pondering;

With slots enough for spying spots
In imagination's play;

A place to hide away at day
Transforms to land of bounty.

A shelter for this city girl
Who's longing for the country;

Lovely world my soul is eying,
Affection not denying.

There is music here of squirrels,
And bees and birds all strumming;

This little city corner yard
My refuge is becoming.

2016

Part III

Awakenings

Part III

Awakenings

Four AM

The clock ticks away
And I am free to think,
Free to listen;
Free to feel;
And no one is chiding me;
Not even the clock on the wall.

2015

Nocturnal Awe

The house is still and silent.
Daytime birds have shut their eyes
And gone to chum in nests;

The noises of the day relent
To ticking of hands clockwise,
And hum of sleepers' rest;

While to my pen and parchment
I send scenes from inner eyes;
And sum of words digested.

At times I have a penchant
To ask, "When does life arise
And come if not invested?"

2017

Dream Away

Cozy bed;
Soft pillow for my head,
I slip away to a dream world,
Where new babes are always born
And where the old never die.

Comfort holds me
In its cradled hand
And rocks me as a child.
Its lullabies it sings to me
In that far off, dreamy land,

Safe and sound
In my internal surreal world
That muffles out distractions all around
And bids me stay awhile, a day—
To play as do the youth.

The hidden land, the unseen world,
Known and then forgotten;
Seen and then veiled to me again;
Remembered not till the next unveiling;
Mystery by day and cloaked in night.

Dream away, dream away
In faraway lands,
Read about in Almanacs,
Pointed to in maps;
Spinning the globe with my finger.

What does one figure—
This storehouse of symbols,
This bed of emotion;
This place of concealed thought
And cognition beyond knowing?

Fly away, fly away;
Take me there upon
The wings of the morning,
The feathers of the dawn
Till I awaken, stretch and yawn.

I say to the Holy One,
"Teach me, teach me;
Instruct me in my sleep;
Speak to me, oh, Heavenly Love;
Carry me on the back of the Dove.

I reach for you, reach for you,
And you reach for me
And find me there,
In my simple humanity,
In my complex design;

In my wistful ramblings,
In my childish mutterings,
In my longingly searching
To touch the hem of your garment;
To see the smile on your face.

Continued...

Meet me there in foggy awareness,
In misty visions of the night;
Meet me under apple trees,
Where I sit at your feet and listen,
Till your words sink to the depth of me.

Take me away, away, away;
Prepare me for the next day.
Sing for me your songs of the night,
That I can sing in the light of the day
And cause me to see in new ways.

Sleep away, sleep away,
In the mist where all cares fade away;
In the midst of luminous ray;
In the deep and the dark of the night,
Help me to live in the day."

2011

Aflame

In the traveling of the night
I saw some faint and distant light
Beckon me into its warm glow;
Draw me into its ever deepening hues
Of reds, yellows, greens and blues,
Dancing in rapid succession;
One tongue lapping and melting into the air,
And then another in unpredictable array
Of measured beat and increasing heat;
But, not an earthly flame was this,
No, something heavenly in this untamed,
Burning zeal that turns sight by faith
Into something tangible and real.

2012

Reflections

All these host on a starry night
Look for the Maker to give them light.
Orion and Neptune cannot compare
To the shine of the One who put them there.
Radiantly, they tell His story.

Naked and feeble we stand below
And look for that One to fill our souls.
From dust we came and to ashes we go;
The days ahead we do not know,
Yet we stand in the glow of His glory.

1997

When Beauty Came

Beauty came and loved me wild
After loving me tame;
Since that magical event in time,
I have never been the same.

In a moment meek and mild—
Like any day mundane—
That chosen day, I became His child,
Though I was always His claim.

2014

Dance of Dawn

He asked to dance with me
Under dark cover of night.
I said, "But I can hardly see."
And He said, "It's alright,
Just come now and dance with me."

He put His hand in mine
Lifting me up from the bed
From where I had been slumbering;
Though sleepy at first, the
Dawn was awakening me.

2013

Dream Dance

With soft warm glow of candlelight
My bed at night receives me with delight.
Dreams wait for me at the precipice of sleep
To meet me in a land of color,
Past the deep, deep dark of night.

There the hidden world within me
Opens up in theatric panoply,
Where actors find their places
Adjust their masks on faces
And play on the stage of my imagination.

Their didactic method
Leaves me lucid and reflective,
As I awaken in the quiet of the night
Or find myself aglow in morning light,
Pondering symbols, meanings, phrases, figures;

Seeking to connect, interpret, reason
With the sub-conscious landscape
Of a slumbering mind.
Dance me, dance me
Into the daylight of the night,

From the land down under
That takes me above the trees,
Over the clouds and to
The starlit sky above
In the circle of the heavens.

Land me in the nations
Far across the sea;
Dance me, dance me there,
While my body lies still in my bed
While my head rests firm on my pillow.

Serenade me with the cello and the lyre;
Let the fire in my soul ignite
The restless fodder of an active mind
To warm and illumine me
For the waking hours.

2013

Prince of Peace

Shalom abides, deep inside;
No one can wrest it from me.
The peace not shallow;

Its girth is wide;
No hollow heart inside,
But hallowed to the Maker;

No subtraction from the mirth
Of the Savior's birth in me,
As repeatedly, He forms His life in me;

And as a vessel on the wheel,
I am created and
Recreated by divine right;

Illumined by heaven's light,
Every night is turned to day,
Yielding to His inscrutable way

Of shalom, shalom, shalom.

2013

In the Spirit

Worship arises,
    Awakened from slumber;
        Bodies start to move;
            Rhythm in the floorboards;
Vibration in the pews;
    Tapping feet, clapping hands,
        Keeping beat;
            Saying good news.
Limbic systems released;
    Synovial fluids flowing
        Dancing breaking out.
            Faces glowing from
Red blood nurturing cells;
    Heart pumping health
        To every member.
            Inhibitions falling with
Human spirits calling out
    To present, accessible,
        Touchable God.
            Glorious experience,
Like waking in a dream,
    But it's real.
        Loosing our masks;
            Finding our smiles;
We'd walk for miles
    To gather again;
        People'd give millions,
            But it's free.

2012

Glory Bourne

Though you're in a mood the lilies still bloom;
The sun still rises in spite of your gloom.
The song birds still flitter on through the noon,
And earth's every critter still breathes deeply
To stay alive.

They cry to you, "Rise up; you will survive!
Awaken inside till you live to thrive!"
Where there is life, there is also hope;
Where there is hope there is courage, so dare
To face the day;

The night fades away and it's brighter still
Around the corner and past the next hill;
There's glory on the summit looking down
And you will see you were not just a clown
For believing.

2015

Life Force

The form will come in creative time;
The dance, the song and the metered rhyme.

It will emerge with its colors bright,
While casting shadows; suffused in light;

Glory of humble; touch of divine
Bottled in human; poured out like wine.

2017

A World Too Small

A world too small is one where you've been before and
You've counted all the specks on the wall and dots on the ceiling.
The air is feeling stuffy, 'cause you're all closed in and
You're looking for a window to pull back the curtains and
Fling open the sash to let the fresh, cool air rush in, along with
The beaming sunlight from the vast open sky. Then you
Look out into the far and wide and say, "That's where
I'm going—way out there." So if the door is blocked
You hatch a plan and concoct how to flee through a window.

A world too small is confinement wall to wall because the world
That has grown within you is larger than it all. You've been there
Before but since gone far beyond, and now you're too tall to fit
Through the door, and have to stoop to come in, and then you
Just want to let yourself out, because you feel like a college grad
Trying to fit in a second grade desk; or an engineer with nothing to
Do but play tic-tac-toe with a four year old. Like when you visit a
High school buddy from forty years before and you're dumbstruck:
They've not changed a stitch, and you can't keep from wilting.

The world inside has become too wide to recede in time to be who
You used to be or live how you used to live or think how you used
To think. It's because you know there's so much more; what used
To be is way too small and there's much less time left than before.
The 70's reruns have seen their day and you can't stand to stay
And flitter the time away because there's just too much at stake.
The person inside can't abide the banal and trite when there's a
River of life, overflowing its banks, that pulls you along, drawing
You in and carrying you far, far away to new places.

2018

Part IV
Apprehended by Truth

Prophesy, Oh Painting

Pig headed people;
Passing polite platitudes;
Presumptuous pragmatisms;
Pretentious pretenders;

Insanity of humbled humanity.
Famous brought low;
Prisoners in a row;
Shackled to each other
Like mismatched brothers.

The greedy feed insatiably
And are not satisfied,
While children play
In blissful ignorance,

Homogenizing commodities
Into bland noodles—no sauce.
Jesus looks on ...
"My sheep, my sheep ...
Have wandered far from me.

2012

This poem was an interpretation of a painting.

The Unseen Friend

He is not far away; he is very near.
Some people can smell him in the air;
He is fragrant—sweet like rose petals.

He feels emotions—like we do.
He gets angry, but the anger passes;
And he never becomes bitter.

The kindest mom, most patient dad
He surpasses; yet he gets a lot
Of bad rap—from wounded people.

We've all done it—shred him with
Our venom; puncture him with holes
Until we draw his blood.

In our anger we pummel him with fists;
We say, "Let me go" and bite his wrists;
And twist the thorns down tighter.

He lets us go, but like a mother hen,
He longs to draw us under strong
Wings and hide us in his feathers;

Like a she bear guarding cubs in
The den. We think he's gone,
But he hovers in the unseen.

He's a convenient scapegoat
For the consequences of
Mankind's stupidity and error;

But still he stands, extends his
Scepter, lends us his hands and
Says, "Please, be my friend."

2017

Inside a Day

Inside a day I saw your kindness,
Gentle as a morning dove.
Inside a day I felt your goodness
And I recognized your great love.

Inside a day the torrents shifted
And calm fell over the land;
Inside a day the storm clouds lifted,
When you cradled me in your hand.

2002

The Stupid Lies I Thought Were True...

That we were placed here randomly by fate;
That my individuality was genetic mistake;
And since there is no destiny at stake,
We only become richer by the things we take...

That life arose from primordial soup
And our value is not much more than poop;
If there's a God, He left us out of the loop;
And we have no more meaning than a hula hoop...

The dogma that we evolved from ape
Which makes us beast from heel to nape;
And we're worth no more than the land we rape;
And God's a fairy tale for children's sake...

That Jesus Christ was just a man
Scraping by in life, as the best of us can,
And somehow maybe we can stand
On the merits of our well intentioned plans...

That man, who is ape, is king by what he takes;
That rape is okay, especially if it makes
Me the author of my own plan;
So whatever it is, for me its grand,

Even if it's nothing more than a scam;
I'll be the woman, (or the man)
That I command myself to be.
And I will do what I damn well please.

We've tried now for a few thousand years,
But maybe someday we'll wipe these tears,
When we finally get over our inborn fears
And get our feeble human act in gear.

Once we cease fighting on this earthly sod,
Perhaps we can prove that we are gods;
That we know best the way to trod—
Though I am Dimbo from the land of Dod.

In evolution's revolving door,
Where future's promise is no more
Than a supposed chain that has no links—
That's the way I was taught to think ...

Before I believed in God.

2014

Commutation

Way up high;
There in the far sky;
Sigh, how I cry;
Too high for me to go.

Oh so low;
A mound for a mole.
With a hole in the soul.
And where does one go?

Last in line
For a meager dole;
Past the given time
For an eager soul.

How to pass
With the sad pilgrim's flight
Through the tough hassle
When the trail is tight?

Harsh with cold;
Frozen in the snow;
Too hard for one to know:
Just how does one sow?

Oh the plight:
Lost in the wind blown,
Dark of stark winter night,
And how will life grow?

How to stay
In the weary fight?
When will new day awake;
Arise from the night?

Way up high;
There in the far sky
To Him I cry;
Too high for me to go.

Oh so low;
He comes down low
To fill my soul;
Where else can I go?

Last in line
For a meager dole
He came just in time
To rescue my soul.

How He passed
On the sad pilgrims side
Through the tough hassle
When the trail was tried.

Harsh with cold
Frozen in the snow
Too hard for one to know
He sowed His own soul.

Oh the delight;
Lost in the wind blown
Dark of stark winter night;
He makes life to grow!

For He stayed
In the weary fight,
Till the new day awoke;
Arisen from night.

2014

Ark

Though I looked there once before,
Now I saw it; an open door.

With the creatures gathered round me,
Wild beasts from near and far,

They were like brothers to me,
With hyena's laugh and lion's roar.

There was no need to fear;
There was an ark and I was here.

For travel's refuge through storm
And wind and rain, I was secure.

2013

Messy Love

Shed abroad—
Fountains of red
Exploding.
Spurting like flares
Into the air
Makes us aware ...

Trumpets blaring;
Are we prepared
For His coming?

... Tears like rivers
Ushered from God
Fall to the ground,
Mingle with sod
To make mud.

Apply to the eyes
Salve for the blind;
Mud in his hand
Health bestowing ...

Embers glowing;
Sir up the fire;
Turn up the heat;
Fan the flame ...
Love is growing ...

No hiding from shame;
No passing the blame;
Guilt washed away
In His name.

Love in His eyes;
Nothing despised
Are His own;
Frozen like stone
Every foe ...

Open the cage;
Release the dove;
Send the calf
In the field
To roam free,
Skipping with glee.

Instead of me,
Scapegoat is led
To the tree.
Barabbas released;
Hanged man is dead.

Lightly, enemy treads–
Afraid of the silence
Locked in a tomb;
Holding his breath,
Fearing that death
Would swoon ...

Stone rolled away

At break of new day;
Headlines make news
For all time:
"No corpse lies here"...

Love paid dearly;
No more suffice—

Yearly sacrifice.
Love bowed low
To enter
Untimely grave ...

Three days to gather
Hell's unsaved.
Earth's forgotten,
Heaven's own ...

Lofty throne;
Nations gather
For the supper
Of the Lamb.

2014

There we stand,

Among the peoples ...
No more "church,"
No steeples; but
All of the redeemed...

All gone before
Seemed like a dream;
It was not real anymore.

Grave is robbed

By God eternal.
Death disrobed of glory;
Ageless story is for real!

Time Traveler

Time Traveler, take me
To the planets spinning in orbit;
To the firmaments parting;
And seas gathering to form dry ground.

Take me to the dawn of earthly time,
When all was fresh and new;
Though no human eye was there,
I would like to witness you.

There, in untouched splendor,
Untrodden purity, like fresh fallen snow
And sands of Sahara undisturbed;
Pristine as Swiss Alps air.

Everywhere, virgin beauty,
Untainted loveliness,
The untamed wild, gentle
And free in holy communion.

There was the union of all
Good and whole; in unstolen love
In trusting innocence;
In childlike joy.

There, was unsoiled earth;
Unpolluted sky;
There were the reasons why
Creator said, "It is good."

All the animals and plant life
Understood their place in Master's plan;
All took their life from His hand;
Harmony was in all the land,

And then... and then came Man...
And he was very good;
Spittin' image of his daddy;
And Pop was proud as punch.

Man—the crown of creation,
Intelligent thinker, capable
Caregiver, given dominion,
Given free will; given the world to rule.

Unspoiled nature from unsullied genes;
Birth without pain; earth without stain of guilt,
Where flowers never wilt; it was
Life before earth went tilt on its axis.

It was maximum good for maximum gain
Before free will chose to rebel against its maker;
Before caregiver became caretaker
Of a hundred billion graves.

And man became the slave of his own greed;
That was before the lie went down deep
And laid its eggs in the heart of man to
Conceive corruption in a thousand untold ways;

That was before man messed up the plan
Because he thought he knew better;
And then, life became bitter
And once sweet souls became sour;

When they no longer had the power
To love as they once could
And they no longer understood
What life was meant to be.   *Continued...*

Time Traveler, I'm not sure I want
To see four thousand years that followed,
Wrought with wars and sorrows,
With worry always for tomorrow;

But take me to the place where time stood still;
Where the curse was reversed; and
Prophesy fulfilled; scripture rehearsed in
Silence was written on the wall.

When all the demons of hell
Stopped short in their applause;
When the tide was turned on them
And a shift echoed in the universe,

As the lamb was shorn, the curtain torn,
And all the angels cheered
Because a path was cleared
Through impossible terrain;

When heaven came to earth;
And a divine dignitary came to reign
And set up an eternal kingdom, unseen by
The worldly wise, but recognized by children;

Then innocence returned
To the hearts of men and women
Who responded to a heavenly call;
And chose the Lover who first loved them.

They are able once again
To stand in human dignity;
To hold their heads up high
And walk without the shame.

As they abide in you, and you in them,

They bear much fruit as they wait
For your appearing, and meanwhile
Bide their time and occupy in its duration.

Time Traveler, let me glimpse the age when
Imps and gargoyles are locked up in a cage;
All the earth will cease to rage against its Maker
And desist in its abhorrence of the Truth;

When all the broken pieces in their stages
Have fitly come together,
And the blueprint of the ages,
Culminates in the final master plan;

When all the wars shall cease;
Over all creation shall rein peace,
And over all the tongues and tribes
Of men will be shalom.

It will be the grand reversal of
The cursed downfall of primal man,
And restoration will be manifest
In earth's entire domain.

The end will be pristine
Like baby earth at its inception
As mankind learns that she was valued,
And treasured since the dawn of time.

We will have chosen the Lover for ourselves
And returned to our rightful place
Because we, who went astray
Are given back our true identity.

Continued...

Time Traveler, take me back to now;
To live today; to see in ways
That give me hope for tomorrow,
For all my sorrows are swallowed up in joy.

I know now that my choice matters;
My decisions last for all eternity.
I was never random chance;
Life was never happenstance;

None of us was a victim of fate.
Now, while it's not too late
To learn to love again,
Help us to live in this current state.

Take us past "somehow to survive"
Or "maybe someday we'll arrive;"
Past all that human effort could contrive;
Past all that we could strive to be but fail.

Help us see beyond the veil; beyond
Ourselves and all the messes and mistakes
We've made along the way
To see that it's a new day.

Time Traveler, take me back to now;
I want to live today, in harmony with you;
To choose to synchronize my will to yours
You're the only door for me.

You've shut the doors of vanity,
And returned me to my sanity.
Now I can take my mantle off the floor
And I can live beyond my history.

"Let's be friends again," I hear you say.
Now, for me there's no other way.
Loving Creator takes me by the hand
So I can stand in present victory.

As was meant from the beginning
For now and all eternity,
Time Traveler, you restore my destiny
As you draw me back to you.

2011

A Painted Poem

The truth, like seeds in capsule form;
Like vitamins, to make one strong;
The hope, that makes one warm inside;
Truth breaking out to reproduce,

From inner place in spirit womb,
Held in winter's secure cocoon,
Kept safe in Abba's hidden place,
Now piercing through with vision eyes,

Truth coming out to take down lies,
While heart is resting, peace inside;
Kept in the cradling hand of God;
Whispering to you His comfort,

And now the hope is birthed anew,
Belief again is coming through;
Still faith is rising up inside,
As Christ is glorified in you.   *2013*

This poem was the interpretation of a painting

Teach Me, Abba

Teach me, Abba, teach me.
I have so much to learn.
Why does the earth on its axis turn?
Why at a tilt? I don't discern.
Why do you light the stars at night so
We visually gather their pinholes of light?
What might the purpose of this be?
Fixed in their orbits, why do planets exist?
What are they for? Maybe a door
Or something more—A mere foyer to
A universe to explore?

Oh Abba, teach me more.
How little does little go—there are so
Many things I do not know,
And in this little mind of mine
You place a child's curiosity.
Life would be a monstrosity
Without you to mentor me.
You were sent to me; to all the world.
We are all in a whirlpool, a tempest,
A storm; then you step on the waves;
You walk on the sea, and so suddenly,

All is well inside of me.
Take my hand, Daddy, for
I am lost, lest you lead me;
I am famished lest you feed me;
Marooned lest you rescue me:
Naked, lest you clothe me in your glory.
Tell me more of your story.
These small eyes of mine

How little do they ever see.
You alone give ability to live my
Individuality. You put in me a prize

And I must dive deep to find it,
As you dive down deep in me,
With laser eyes of purity that cut away
The cancer in my soul. Your piercing eyes
Look into mine and make me whole.
As a child I bounce on your knee
And I exuberantly decree, "You are my
Daddy; always, I am your little girl."
Catch me in your whirlwind of affection;
Spin me out in every direction, 'til
I am dizzy in the knowledge of your love.

Teach me, Abba, Teach me;
There is so much I want to know.
Show me how the grasses grow
As they blow like waves of the sea.
Something in me must grow also—not
Content with bent of crooked yesterdays,
While the best days are ahead of me;
You grant me live in the pleasure of now.
Somehow, I don't know how—
You always make a way for me.
Abba, dear Abba, help me to see

The vision that you have for me.
Make of me all you intend for me to be.
Then I will really be free;

Continued...

Released in true liberty.
Yes, Abba, take me here and there,
And go with me everywhere;
That is always where I want to be.
Abba, Abba – You and me.
… But, but, what of these – all these
People you put around me?
How do I begin to know what love means,

Unless you instruct me?
So very easily I offend, and as
Easily offence is brought to me.
How do we live in harmony?
How do we cope with one another;
To love our sisters and brothers?
We keep stepping on each others' toes—
And that is only the first of so many woes
That we bring upon ourselves.
Oh Abba, How do we know how to love,
Except You show us what love does?

We are very small containers—
Embarrassing how little we hold.
Why is it so difficult for us to behold?
Why do we let minute matters
Blur the sight of the essential?
Or dwarf each other in our potential; to
Hold each others' hands and work together?
Why do we argue insignificant scraps,
And snap at slight irritations?
Or wrap our friends in cellophane
And gag them with rags of blame?

Why do we shoot shame in flames of rage?
We need a sage to teach us better ways,
Begging a cure to heal our bitter days.
Oh Abba, we are needy for your love.
Take us past our own wit's end;
Teach us to operate in your system,
Far above our grimy, filthy fare.
Help us dare to trust you;
Give us courage to believe
That what you say is true.
Readjust us so we function like you.

Realign us with your properties,
As you align the planets and stars
In the heavens afar; so realign us
Where we are, right here, right now.
Help us to bow to your sovereignty
Power us to pray, "Christ reign in me."
Let every human under heaven say
"Your Kingdom come in me.
Your will be done in me." Let
Love compel us to heed your call,
As you teach us Abba, one and all.

2013

Two Trees

Stay away from the poison
Of the Negativa Tree.
Its bark makes you itchy
And then you feel its bite.
The itch makes you scratch
For an iffy sales pitch;
"If only, If only"
Is its vanity wish;

For it's always better
On the other side
Of the Negativa Tree;
And all the scratch'n
Makes more itch a hatch'n
And you're never satisfied.
Then, the bite of bad fruit—
A big chunk of your life
Misinvested in lies by
The Negativa Tree worm.

You will wiggle and squirm
When it's under your skin;
Your patience will wear thin,
And your prospects look dim,
Even when the sunshine's
Streaming in from the sky;
You'll just complain that
It's blinding your eyes.

Its flower is deception
And its fragrance is fraud;
But its sap makes you cuddle
On the devil's lap, till

You awake from the stupor,
Feeling like a loser,
Huddled in a corner,
And you think you're all alone.

But, don't give up hope!
There is an antidote
For the Negativa Tree.
A tree of another variety, the
Zoe Tree grows on the riverside.
Emitting fragrance far and wide,
From blossoms of promise
That bloom in the spring;

Its leaves are for healing;
Its bark makes sweet tea;
On its branches many birds sing;
But this is a most marvelous thing:
Fruit ripens all year round;
Another most amazing fact—
To make up for all you've lacked—
Its delectables are of
Every kind; those with

Skin and those with rind—
Beyond the thinking of the
Most imaginative mind—
All of it sweet to the eater
And good for the taste.
A balm for the human race,
It is the nations' delight.
It is the true soul food,
That makes the body whole.   *Continued...*
It makes the eyes bright,

The thoughts clear,
The thinking right.
It is heaven's seed for
The human breed.
Try it, and you will see;
Taste it, 'cause its free; come,
Partake of the Tree of Life.

2014

#1 Toxic Thought:, "I Am Not Loved"*

Stay out of trouble;
Don't get caught in the rubble;
Be loosed from the muddle
Of a toxic thought.
Throw it in the trash heap;
Cast it in the fire;
Annihilate the dire talk;
Toss it in the mire.
Say, "It is not true"
And, "No, I don't believe it;
Refuse to receive it,
'Cause it's not good for you!
Don't believe it
Or receive it;
Don't tinker with it
Or play with it;
Or give it any space.
It's from an alien race;
Not fit for human consumption;
Not compatible to human hearts
Or designed for human minds.
Say, "It does not compute,"
Delete, delete the same
And do not repeat the refrain.
Get off the danger train;
It's a deadly flu strain,
Because it is not true.
So muster all your courage,
And gather all your faith
And say with total confidence,
"I'm loved, and that's the truth!"

2014

And It Was So

God said, "Let there be light" and it was so, and it was good; He
Made the moon to rule the night and the sun to waken the day...
Let there be plants and flowers; trees that tower and bear fruit,

Each from seeds after their kind, and it was so and it was good...
Let living creatures fill the air and seas, and wild beasts to roam
The land; each after its own kind, and it was so, and it was good...

And He formed Adam from the dust and breathed life into his
Nostrils. Then from his rib, He fashioned Eve; thus He said and
This He did, and it was so, and they were good....

God said to all His living beings, "Multiply and fill the earth, each
After your own kind;" your own kind; your own kind.
Thus God said and this He did, and it was so, and it was all good...

After the dreadful fall, God made a way to preserve all their kinds
And all their seeds, so as to save His beloved creation...
He told Noah, "Build an ark" and Noah did, just as God said;

And the animals came, two of each kind, of each kind, of each
Kind, so that after the flood they would again multiply and fill the
Earth, each after their own kind, their own kind, their own kind.

Thus God said and this He did and it was so and it was good.
This is history; this is science; this is truth, for God does not lie.
He is the inventor of history and the designer of science,

He is the author of all truth; the giver of all life.
He told us how He made the world so we would know;
Each after our own kind, He told us to multiply and fill the earth.

He told us how so we would know; so we would know. Let It be understood that God is truthful and God is good; So He Spoke and so He did; and it was so, and it was so, and it is so.

2017

Spirit Journey

There's a better way to live, I heard,
Though in my blindness it seemed absurd,
For I could not find a trail to wind
Through the tangled jungle in my mind.
It seemed life would leave me behind;
That I would sit weeping evermore
On some windy God-forsaken shore,

Thinking that I missed my ship.
For I'd always make a regretful slip,
In my silly attempt to be princess.
I knew I was in a pitiful mess
And I couldn't have felt less
Like some sought after treasure;
Not in my own meager measure.

The weight was too heavy to bear;
My soul sickness I could not share,
As I carried the travel-weary pain
Of a vision I could never attain,
And I felt all hope in me drain;
My life fell apart at the seams …
But now it all now seems like a dream,

Since that day long years ago,
When I met the Captain of my soul,
Who said I was not past my prime,
Nor did I miss my window of time;
This was a day of joy sublime
To begin on my spirit journey,
Where I could begin to be me.

2015

Free of the Web

I was lured into a web
By the words I spoke.
I was caught in a web
That strangled hope.

I was snared in a web
Of self-pity and mope;
Stuck fast in a web
Of my own making,

Clenched teeth grinding;
Closed fists pounding;
Frustration seething;
My words complaining,

Binding my will; web of
Worry, gluey verbiage;
Sticky mess; strings attached,
Stretched across my mass of mind;

Distracting me on every side;
Blurring my wide vision;
Blocking my hearing ears;
Crippling my mobility;

Fogging my ability to think;
Bound in a straight- jacket
Of my own undertaking,
Every surly word making it worse!

Continued...

To be loosed I had to use
My words—sharp truth swords;
Clean words, strong words—
To dismantle the cords;

Slashing through fibers,
One by one, two by two,
Till they were all cut through,
Severed, every last one.

Envy, jealousy, wounded pride—
All of the ego trip jammed up inside,
Held in tight bows of petty
Ribbons—now released!

To the floor fall the fetters;
Clank! go the chains. The web?
The web is dead: spun by words
And killed by the same, just

Rearranged in right order;
Put though the sorter to
Come out true; no leaky
Sewage seeping through.

I changed my verse to
Reverse the curse, and the
Blessings unwound me,
Unbound me from their hold;

Rescued from the web
Of the spider's stronghold
When truth cut the lines
And delivered my soul.

I gave myself hope
Through the words I spoke
And I became bold
By the truth I told myself.

It was the truth I believed,
That liberated me;
They were the words
That set my heart free.

2017

Part V

In the Light of His Glory

The Giving Well

It's hot in the furnace
For the compromised soul;
It's hot in the furnace,
But it is not hell.

It's tight in the middle
Of a locked-up cell.
It's tight in the riddle,
But it is not hell.

It is well for the winner
Who awaits his goal;
It is well for the sinner
Who escapes his hell.

It is good for the giver
Who loves us well;
It is good for the living
To give as well.

It is the Life-Giver
Who mends our souls;
To make us life-livers
Who love as well.

I don't like the furnace
Or the locked-up cell,
But I'm here for the giving
And I'm giving well.

There's joy in the giving
For a living soul;
There's joy in the living,
And I'm living well.

There's grace for the giver
Who tends his soul;
There's peace like a river
And a living well.

There's love for the living
Who spend their souls;
There's heaven inside
And a giving well.

2014

In Praise of Christ

You are the promised treasure,
With value beyond all measure.
You are the pearl of greatest price;
You are the most coveted prize.

What can compare to knowing you,
And how can mere words describe
The presence of your Kingdom here;
The glory where you reside?

That you come down from Heaven
And enter this prodigal earth;
Mingling with sons and daughters of men,
Pouring out mercy for everyone.

What boundless love is this,
To go to such extremity;
To pay the utmost cost for me;
To bear my debt upon that tree?

How can our small hearts express
Such boundless gratitude?
How can our meager lives repay
Such generous magnitude?

No adequate way of giving thanks,
But we offer ourselves to you.
To say, "Here I am. Have your way.
Let our lives be worship every day."

Please make your home inside,
Forming us as vessels of clay;
Transforming us every day;
And ordering our human ways.

May our hearts turn toward you;
And all our thoughts include you.
That all our ways ordered by you;
And all our delight found in you.

2006

I Will Praise

When the morning falls on the farthest hill,
I will praise His name; I will praise;

For the Lord our God—He is strong to save
From the arms of death; from the deepest grave.

He gave as He lived in His perfect will,
And by His grace, I will praise Him still.

1999

Pray!

Pray in quiet and pray in noise.
Pray in silence and pray with voice.
Pray in English and pray in tongues.
Pray in whispers and pray with lungs!

Pray in weakness and pray in strength.
Pray in shortness and pray in length.
Pray in laughter and pray through tears;
In the moment and through the years.

Pray in sorrow and pray in praise;
In the night and through the days.
Pray in solitude and in the crowd;
Pray with music and sing out loud!

Pray through scripture and speak the Word;
Pray in assembly and one accord.
Pray in poetry and through the Psalms.
Pray with gifts while giving alms.

Pray in pictures and while you write.
Pray in faith till you find delight.
Pray in the dance with all your might;
Just watch God set things aright!

Pray in brokenness and on the mend.
Pray over letters you're going to send.
Pray over needs of those you love
With the guidance of the Holy Dove.

Pray while you walk and keeping pace;
Pray till every barren place
Is touched with heavenly grace;
Every negativity with joy replaced!

Pray through sickness and pray in health.
Pray in poverty and pray in wealth.
Pray though hunger and be satisfied;
Pray forgiveness; be rectified.

Pray for enemies and for your friends;
Pray for borrowers and they that lend.
Pray for the bullies and for the wise guys.
Pray in faith and see with new eyes.

Pray for strangers and those you know.
Pray at home and every place you go;
Pray for family and pray for foe;
Pray for the healing of every woe.

Pray through darkness till you see the light;
Pray in blindness till you find your sight.
Pray in frailty till you feel His might
Pray through wrongs till all is right.

Pray until your soul is fed;
Pray until you know you're led.
Pray until the doubt is dead;
And the arch enemy has fled.

Persevere with firm resolve
To believe for problems solved;
Until your soul has found release;
Pray till you know Shalom Peace.

Pray till you rest in Abba's arms,
Knowing you're safe from all alarm;
Til every storm has turned to calm;
Wave your palms! Pray "Hosannah!"

2014

I Testify

How fine, how fine
Was this time on the earth
For you've redeemed all things
    All things, all things;
And they're all working together for good,
So I live in the neighborhood
Where peace and joy are mine…
    Oh love divine!
        Oh holy wine is mine,
            Is mine!
For there is a life within me
Of another kind
Mined in the mountains of gold.

Your Spirit is anointing me to see
The wonder of your loveliness.
What bliss, oh what bliss is mine!
What call divine to be more than your servant;
Even your child;
What wild imagination could have conceived this?

All the fear from yesteryear can be dismissed.
I never need miss this bus again,
And when I've reached my destination,
I'll look back and relay
The greatest story ever told;

That's real; the real deal;
That makes children squeal with delight.
I laugh with all my might,
For crying's done in the night;
Now it's all right,
All right with me.

I'm free,
For the greatest thing in history
Is knowing you,
And you know me
And love me too;
Love me true.
Yes you do, always.

Distracting devotions are hatching a worm,
But don't squirm;
Meet Him on His terms.
Let Him hold you firm and steady;
He will make you ready.
Lean on Him and
He will make your dreams come true.
He's watching over you

Every lesser thing is moot;
But His promises are true.
Listen and you will hear Him.
Let Him kiss you under the mistletoe.
He won't go away,
So never throw your hopes away.

He was your scapegoat,
Who took your place,
And He will help you run the race,
Till you cross the finish line—
Just in time,
       Just in time
              To win.
Now you can wear that grin.   *Continued...*

He holds you safely in His hand;
It's a grand, grand plan;
He makes us one new man,
So lift your eyes, child,
And let Him in to stay!

2011

Bring Your Offerings

Bring your offerings
Dance; sing; play your strings;
Do most anything.
Give toast to the King;
The most you can bring.

Host angel beings
Watch heavenly sightings;
Join choral singing;
Full hearts are bringing
All praise to the King!

Don't say it's not enough;
Not big enough;
Not good enough;
Bring your gifts to the altar
And lay them down.

Do you know I have a gown
And a crown
Set aside just for you?
I've given you a job to do
And that's my joy for you.

Live the heart I've given you;
Just do the best
That you can do;
I'll do the rest.
I'll add my magic to the stew
As I partner with you.

Together we'll make music;
The painting;
The sculpture too.
Together we'll dance
To Timbuktu;
And you'll be so very happy
When you do!

2013

Oh, For the Love of God

Oh for the love of God to consume me.
Break out great love; through jealousy,
Heaviness, sadness and fear;
Break out for people far and near;
Break out as I meet with those on the streets.
May your Spirit fill my hands and feet;
Overcome me from my head to my toe;
Cover each heartache and every woe;
Embrace me till the warmth removes all chill;
Infuse me with delight to do thy will.

2004

All for the Glory of God

You would clip our wings, but
We've got to fly, to soar to the sky.
These butterflies won't fit inside
The small cocoons of yesterday;
They are way too small, too small, too small!

You cannot fathom why,
But we are too young to die
In a place too small for us;
We are too old to lie
About a dream alive, alive, alive in us!

It's so hard to say goodbye,
Especially when you won't see why,
As you do not understand
This woman and this man,
Nor comprehend the gifts, the gifts, the gifts we bring!

Still, we dance, we sing;
Still we bring our offerings
To Christ, our Lord and King,
Who sees and knows all things, all things, all things!
Adieu, Adieu, beloveds!

His foundation we depend upon.
His call can't be denied,
Upwards we must fly and forward go
It is the hand, the hand, the hand,
Of God that leads us on!

Out of this familiar boat
Unto waves where feet don't float,
To walk with shoes of faith not fate.
He closes doors to open gates.
And through those gates we follow, follow, follow!

Some day you'll see us, and not shallow;
Someday you'll know us, and not fallow;
Why we had to leave you, though not bitter;
Why we had to go, all for the better, better, better!
Adieu, adieu, our Kingdom fellows,

All for the glory of God!

Sometimes we need take our leave of people we love, because in some way or another, we will become stagnant if we stay,

2015

What Kind of Love?

What kind of love is this?
That He gives us His name ...
To heal the sick,
Comfort the troubled,
Give hope to the hopeless,
And we use it as a curse word.

That He calls us but we don't listen;
He draws us but we resist Him;
That He tells us the truth,
Yet we don't believe it;
And opens wide His arms,
But we don't come.

That He created the universe,
But we don't give Him credit
For His own art; saying
That it randomly evolved.
Yet He esteems us, telling
Us we are worth His while.

We fail Him again and again,
But He doesn't give up on us;
We grieve His heart but
He continues to forgive us.
We don't give Him the time of day,
While He patiently waits for us.

Though we be stricken
With our own wrongs,
He does not condemn us;
And though we may reject Him,
He does not reject us;
Nor does His heart grow cold.

Though we are faithless,
He stays committed to us.
Though stuck in our sin,
And or lost in our way;
He's there for us night and day
And His love does not grow dim. ...

Oh my, what kind of love is this?

2014

Life inside Christ

I've got freedom that touches the skies;
I've got freedom that glows in my eyes;
I've got freedom that others can't see
In this world inside me.

I've got hope that sorrow can't quench;
I've got hope that gives instead of lends;
I've got hope that stays my fears;
And dries my every tear.

I've got love that heals my wounds;
I've got love that romances the moon;
I've got love that waters my soul;
And gives each day a goal.

I've got peace that caresses the breeze;
I've got peace that lives in ease;
I've got peace that is my wealth;
And brings my body health.

I've got life that death can't kill;
I've got life that God can fill;
I've got life that holds a prize;
It's life inside of Christ.

2016

Providence Beckons Me

In the ordinary,
Opportunity knocks,
So I open a window
And a door unlock...
    While Providence beckons me...

Massage for my husband;
For my son a good deed;
Laughter in friendship;
Helping a neighbor in need;

Adoring my grandson,
Who I hold in my arms;
Affirming a poet,
I would shield her from harm.

Routine wrapped in purpose;
Clothed in noble destiny;
Mundane finely arrayed,
Counts for eternity...
    For Providence beckons me...

Combined in good order,
All is meant for a reason;
As I sweep the floor, or
Plant flowers in season.

In a myriad of ways;
While love ebbs and flows,
I experience my days
Till for me the bell tolls;

Reading books through the hours,
Learning more every day;
Encountering truth from our
Forgotten olden ways;

Friendly smile; fond kiss;
Hearty hug for another;
Every note, card, good wish
Makes its mark forever...
    As Providence beckons me...

Every "Hello," "Good bye,"
Playful tickle; silly smile;
Winsome wink of the eye;
Invites the love inside;

From Cupid's bow, no dart,
But further, higher arc;
Past trappings, to the heart;
Straight to target, hits its mark;

Healing arrow throwing;
Wrapped in goodness, flowing;
Trusting beyond knowing
And loving beyond fear.

Minutes, days, months, years—
A journey kept for a soul;
Stored in memory tears;
Prepares a heavenly home...
    When Providence beckons me.

2016

Wellspring

There's love that goes deeper than death;
And a friend closer than my breath

Who fills the hollow place in me.
Joy bells on feet, He visits me.

Though I have not a claim to fame—
He seeks me out and calls my name.

And though I feel dull, small and weak,
He gives to me a voice to speak.

He wants to keep me company.
He's here for me with empathy.

For every life lesson to learn,
He's given me eyes to discern.

He brings healing for every tear,
Through all the seasons of the year.

He's with me in the midst of all;
Through spring, summer, winter, and fall;

Though I know I am not worthy,
He includes me in his story;

Little me his love sought after –
He, the wellspring of my laughter.

2015

Forgiven

My sins are washed away: I wear a robe
White as wool; clean as fresh fallen snow,
Just as they say: all the stain down the drain;
Left on the last train to hell while my soul is heaven-bound.

I was lost, completely lost; now I'm gloriously found.
I may stand on the ground but my spirit soars; my
Reward is in heaven—my reward worth waiting for;
The door is open; my chains are broken;

My Advocate has spoken for me and I am free.
He met the fee; He paid the price; no more
Chance or dice in this life; no more strife or worry;
No more rush and hurry; no more stress of

Fretful scurry to try to make things right.
It's all been done for me; now I have only to live free.
What can a person say? For all the nights and days
My God has made a way for me—sweet liberty!

So how now can I say anything other than "I forgive,
I let you go; I let you live; I pardon and release"?
There is no grief in giving grace; no sorrow looking
In the face: no shame to chase the joy away;

No stolen toy from any girl or boy; no lost
Destiny for any woman or man; stand, stand:
Stand free, stand tall; stand one and all who
Hear the call and say, "Yes" to the King, who's

Continued...

Robed in white, light shining from His eyes; life
Beaming liberty on all the sons and daughters of men;
As we are forgiven, so we forgive and forgive again;
And live and live and live free for all eternity!

2017

Perichoresis

No longer just me, poor me;
Walk by me; leave me
Unnoticed; weak- kneed;
Feeble in my estimation.

No longer, "nobody;" no more
And never evermore;
Living death went out the door
As well as dying life.

I am not a wife to poverty;
I am not an heir to sin
Since my Savior knocked
And said, "Let me in."

Who I was before is
Historical lore;
Now I am present
And so much more.

I am not just me; I am in
You; and You in me;
Together somehow in
Mystery, there is a trinity,
And in this I am whole—

My true identity; never more
To see myself alone; my
Lord is on the throne

And I am seated there
With Him, far above
Constraints of little man
Or little woman; my heart

Emboldened to the chiding
Of the enemy, because
I am abiding in the Tree
Of Life and the Tree of Life

Abides in me; I am free;
Here is liberty; Here I am
True me; all I was designed
To be. Seed of woman and

Sperm of heaven combined
To join Celestial with humanity;
To create one New Man—
New Adam and New Eve.

Here is blossom for beauty;
Leaves for healing; fruit for
Eating: abiding in the Vine;
Living in the Tree of Life, beyond

All strife because I am in You and
You are in me; together we are three;
Three in one and one in three; this
Is the life for me—Perichoresis.   *2017*

Other Books in the Circles of Grace Series

The Looking Glass is a selection of poems about perception, more specifically, how one interprets past experiences; how we see ourselves; how we perceive but also misperceive other people, and how those misperceptions can be corrected. I believe that within my own limited perceptions, misperceptions and self-corrections, I speak of universal phenomena.

In the chapter, "Celebrating People," I have chosen to affirm specific individuals of the qualities I see in them and to call forth the potential I believe them to possess. This is something we can all do to empower one another.

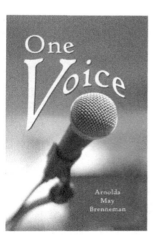

One Voice – We all have been given a voice; we each have one voice to speak during our lifetime. What is it we each want to speak to the world? We speak with the words we say and write; we speak through our art. We also speak with our lives, as the saying goes, "actions speak louder than words."

There are many whose voices have been silenced. There are those who want to speak but have not been able to find their voice. Perhaps they felt they did not have the right to speak or the freedom to do so.

As our brothers' keepers we can choose to help others find their voice, and sometimes, if they cannot speak, to give them voice through our words.

More Books by Arnolda May Brenneman
Order all books online at amazon.com

The Stepping Stones Series

* Awakened to Wonder
* Along the Journey
* Loving Through the Seasons of Life
* Kingdom Living
* To Life!

Children's Poetry Series

* It's A Beautiful World
* When Life is Hard
* Rainbows are for Promises Kept